Linking art to the world around us

artyfacts

Light and Colour

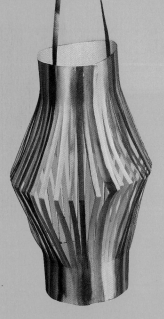

CONCEPT

Publisher: Felicia Law

Design: Tracy Carrington

Editorial Planning: Karen Foster

Research and Development: Gerry Bailey, Alec Edgington

PROJECT DEVELOPMENT

Project Director: Karen Foster

Editors: Claire Sipi, Hazel Songhurst, Samantha Sweeney

Design Director: Tracy Carrington

Design Manager: Flora Awolaja

Design and DTP: Claire Penny, Paul Montague, James Thompson, Mark Dempsey

Photo and Art Editor: Andrea Sadler

Illustrator: Jan Smith

Model Artist: Sophie Dean

Further models: Sue Partington, Abigail Dean

Digital Workflow: Edward MacDermott

Production: Victoria Grimsell, Christina Brown

Scanning: Acumen Colour Ltd

Published by Abbey Children's Books
(a division of Abbey Home Media Group)

Abbey Home Media Group
435-437 Edgware Road
London W2 1TH
United Kingdom

© 2002 Abbey Home Media Group plc

Printed and bound by Dai Nippon, Hong Kong

Linking art to the world around us

artyfacts
Light and Colour

Contents

WRITTEN BY Barbara Taylor

Bright colours

MIXING COLOURS

Primary colours can be mixed in different combinations to produce almost any other colour. When two primary colours are mixed together, the new colour is called a secondary colour. Red and yellow, for example, can be mixed to make the secondary colour orange.

PRINTING PRIMARIES

Red, blue and yellow are the primary, or basic colours most used by artists. However, for printing, another group of basic colours is used: magenta (a purplish-red colour), cyan (bluish-green) and yellow. In both cases, the three basic colours will produce many other colours when they are mixed together.

SHADES, TINTS AND TONES

If you combine the three primary colours, you get a colour that is almost black. Better blacks are produced by adding a powder called 'carbon black'. Mixing black with a colour creates a 'shade'. Mixing white with a colour creates a 'tint'. Mixing grey with a colour creates a 'tone'.

LIGHT PRIMARIES

Different colours of light also combine to produce new colours. Red, blue and green are primary colours in light. If you mix pure red and pure green light, you get yellow light. If you mix all three primaries you can get white light, which appears to have no colour at all.

When you look around you, especially on a sunny day, you can see many different colours and different shades of colour. Some flowers are red, the sky is blue and the sun is yellow. These three strong colours, red, blue and yellow, are called primary colours.

Bold mosaics

Choose strong colours for a really brilliant look!

Colour

WHAT YOU NEED

gluestick

ruler

pencil

scissors

backing card

coloured paper

1 Using a ruler and pencil, draw small squares on sheets of coloured paper and cut them out.

2 Sketch a design, then arrange the squares in a mosaic pattern on backing card.

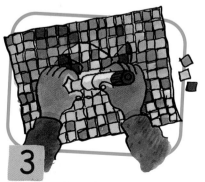

3 Glue the squares to the card to complete your mosaic.

4 You could use this method to make any kind of picture. Stick the coloured card into the different areas to colour in your scene.

Sunshine

The Sun is the nearest star to the Earth. It gives off light and heat because it is a whirling cloud of very hot gases, which glow very brightly. Even though the Sun is 150 million kilometres from the Earth, light from the Sun reaches the Earth in only eight minutes! This is because the light travels at an amazing 330 million metres every second.

LIGHT FOR LIFE

Without the light and warmth from our Sun, there would be no life on Earth. Plants use the Sun's light energy to make their own food. This process is called photosynthesis, which means 'making things with light'. Many plants, such as sunflowers, even turn to face the Sun as it moves across the sky during the day.

DAY AND NIGHT

Even though the Sun looks as though it moves up in the sky during the day and sinks down again at night, it is really the Earth that is moving, not the Sun. The Earth spins around once every 24 hours. When your part of the Earth turns towards the Sun, it looks as if the Sun is rising and the day starts. When your part of the Earth turns away from the Sun, the Sun disappears and darkness falls. The Earth spins eastwards, which is why the Sun appears to rise in the east and set in the west.

SHADOW CLOCKS

Sundials were invented about 2,800 years ago in Egypt. As the Sun shines on a stick, called a gnomon, a shadow is cast on a dial marked in hours. As the Sun moves across the sky, the shadow moves around the dial – like the hands that move around a clock.

Sunflowers turn their heads to follow the light and warmth of the Sun

Golden sundial

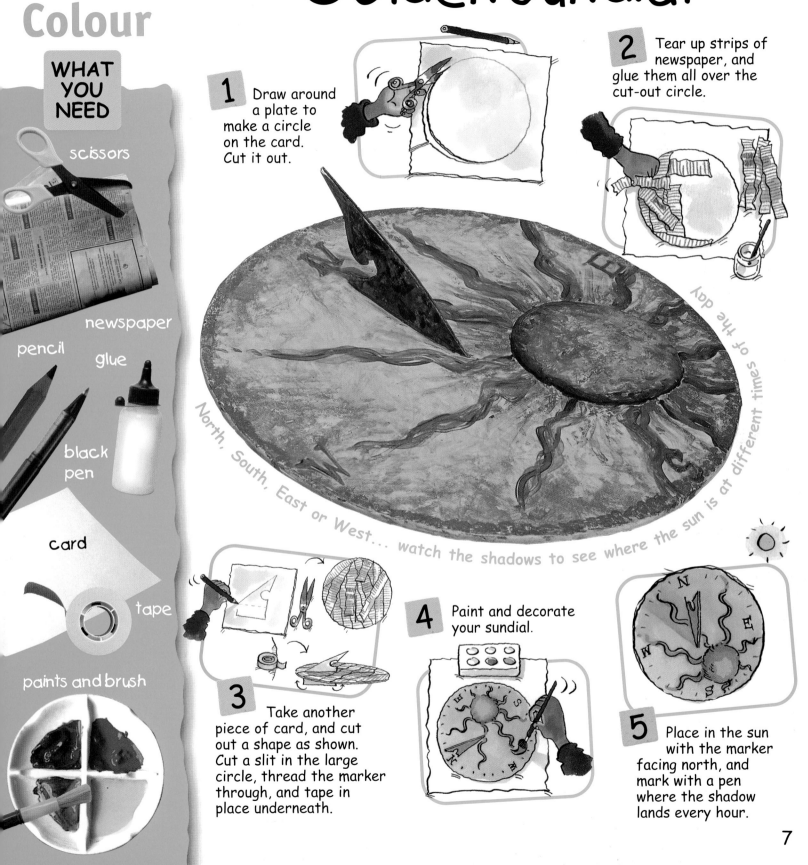

Colour

WHAT YOU NEED

scissors

newspaper

pencil

glue

black pen

card

tape

paints and brush

1 Draw around a plate to make a circle on the card. Cut it out.

2 Tear up strips of newspaper, and glue them all over the cut-out circle.

North, South, East or West... watch the shadows to see where the sun is at different times of the day.

3 Take another piece of card, and cut out a shape as shown. Cut a slit in the large circle, thread the marker through, and tape in place underneath.

4 Paint and decorate your sundial.

5 Place in the sun with the marker facing north, and mark with a pen where the shadow lands every hour.

7

Silvery shades

When a shoal of fish turns quickly,
its sides flash silver to confuse its enemies.

When you look down into a murky stream or river, it is often difficult to see the fish that live there. Sometimes you spot a glint of sparkling silver, or a shadow gliding beneath the surface. The fish have special colouring that helps them to stay hidden from watching eyes. The top side of the fish is dark grey or green, while the under side is white or silver. This colouring is a mixture of light and dark, called countershading.

SAFETY IN NUMBERS

A shoal might be made up of thousands of fish. Travelling together in a group gives small fish protection from their enemies. A predator finds it much more difficult to single out and catch one fish swimming in such a large group.

COUNTERSHADING IN SHOALS

The shoal also uses light, shade and colour to protect itself from attack by bigger fish, such as sharks and rays. When the predator comes close by, the shoal turns away sharply from its enemy. Sunlight glints off the silver sides of the fish, causing a sudden flash of light. This flash confuses the predator just long enough for the shoal to escape. Other kinds of fish protect themselves from attack in different ways. Some are patterned or coloured to blend in with their surroundings or the ocean floor. Some have sharp spines with poisonous tips growing from their sides or tail.

Colour

Flashing fish

Make a swimming shoal of silvery shining fish

WHAT YOU NEED

- scissors
- silver paper
- glue
- pencil
- double-sided tape
- white card
- string
- black paper
- wire
- brush
- black paint
- silver paint

1 Fold a piece of card in half, draw a fish shape and cut it out.

2 Paint one half black. Cut circles from the silver paper and glue them on.

3 Using silver paint, paint a face and lines on the tail and fins.

4 Paint the other half silver and decorate in the same way with black circles and paint.

5 Stick the fish sides together using double-sided sticky tape.

6 Make a circle with the wire. Tie on four long pieces of string. Knot them together so that your mobile can hang from the ceiling.

7 Attach a piece of thread to the fish's fin and tie the other end of it to the wire circle. Now add more fish to your mobile.

9

Reflections

When you look in the mirror, you see a reflection of yourself. This is because light bounces off the mirror into your eyes, rather like a ball bouncing off a wall. Reflections are caused by light bouncing off things. Most things reflect light in some way. Look at the reflection of the Indian palace, the Taj Mahal, in the water. When the water ripples, the mirror image of the Taj Mahal ripples too.

Mirror Images

Mirrors produce very good reflections because they are smooth and shiny and reflect most of the light that shines on them. They are made of sheets of glass with a silvery coating on the back. Your reflection in a mirror seems to be behind the mirror. But if you look behind the mirror, your reflection is not there!

It just appears to be the same distance behind the mirror as you are in front of it. A mirror image is called a virtual, or unreal, image. Another odd thing about your reflection is that left and right are reversed. If you touch your right ear, your reflection touches its left ear and if you touch your left ear, your reflection does the opposite.

Curved mirrors

Curved mirrors change the size and shape of things reflected in them. A spoon is a sort of curved mirror. The front of the spoon curves inwards. This is called a concave surface and it makes your reflection look upside down! The back of a spoon curves outwards in a convex shape. Your reflection looks the right way up, but smaller. Fairground mirrors curve in and out to distort the reflections of people and make them look very funny – stretched out in some places and squashed in others.

Mirror ball

Colour

WHAT YOU NEED

paint and brush

sequins

newspaper

ball

glue

string

skewer or similar instrument

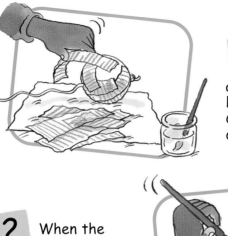

1 Ask an adult to make a hole in the ball, and thread a length of knotted string through it. Cover the ball with pieces of glued newspaper.

2 When the newspaper is dry, paint the ball a bright colour.

3 Glue sequins of different sizes all over the ball until it is covered.

4 Hang from the ceiling or in the window to see it catch the light and produce reflections.

Hang your mirror ball so it shines and reflects light. Brilliant!

11

Metallic gleam

CHANGING COLOURS

As time goes by, the colour of gold stays the same, but the colour of most other metals can change. For example, the metal iron turns orangey-red with rust when it gets wet. Unless silver is kept polished, it turns black when it is exposed to the air for a long time. To stop this colour change, silver is often mixed with other metals.

SHINY THINGS

Many of the ordinary things we use every day are made of silvery, polished metals, such as steel or chrome. We can write messages with colourful metallic inks, and paint our nails with gleaming metallic nail varnish. Cars are often painted with a special metallic paint to give them a smooth, glossy coating.

GLITTERING STARS

Famous film actors or pop stars, when they perform on stage, often gleam and glitter in eye-catching outfits, made from colourful, metallic fabrics and shining metal jewellery. When we want a party or other celebration to be extra-special, we hang up silver and gold-coloured decorations. And we also give gleaming gold, silver and bronze medals as prizes at sports events, such as the Olympic Games.

Objects made from metal, or covered with a metallic coating, usually have a smooth surface, making them shine. This is because the light reflects straight off the surface, quickly filling our eyes. A rough surface scatters the light, so that less reaches our eyes, making an object look dull. The metallic picture above has a variety of polished surfaces. These reflect light in different directions, resulting in a geometric pattern.

Colour

Glitter lab

WHAT YOU NEED

paints and brush

bubble wrap

paper and card

sequins

scissors

straws

foil

silver and copper paper

cellophane

glue

glitter

1 Cut out and paint different shapes representing tubes and glass jars from card.

2 Line them up and stick them onto a piece of paper.

3 Glue onto the tubes and jars straws, sequins, glitter, different see-through plastics and metallic papers.

How many metallic textures can you add to your lab?

PVA

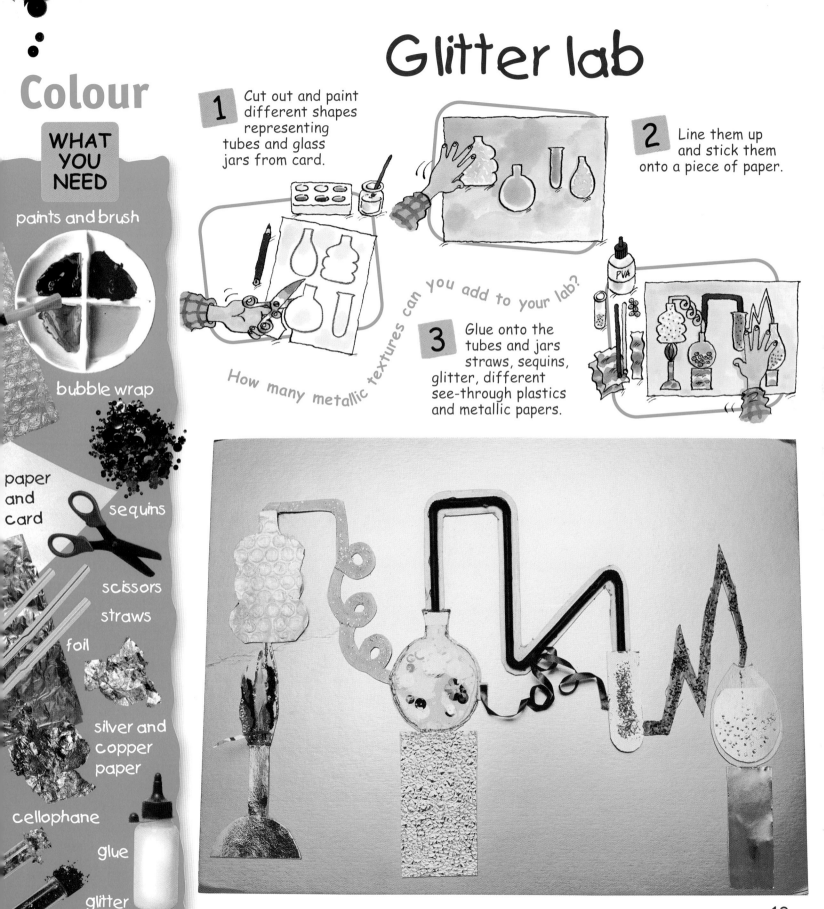

13

Skylights

Far away from the equator, near the North and South poles, a spectacular light show sometimes appears in the sky. It is called an aurora – another word for 'dawn'. Auroras can only be seen at night, and appear as arcs, clouds or streaks that move, brighten, or flicker across the sky.

COLOURED LIGHTS

Auroras are usually green, but those that appear very high in the sky may be red or purple. Most auroras shine about 100 to 1,000 kilometres above the Earth, and some can stretch for thousands of kilometres.

SKY BLUE

Have you ever wondered why the sky is blue and sometimes other colours? It is because the different rainbow colours of sunlight – red, orange, yellow, green, blue, indigo and violet – are scattered in all directions as they bounce off the dust and water particles in the Earth's atmosphere. Blue and violet light are easily scattered by the particles. Red light scatters the least. When you look at the sky on a clear day, you see lots of scattered blue light, making the sky appear blue.

PAINTED SUNSETS

At sunrise and sunset, the Sun is low in the sky. The sunlight has to travel farther before it reaches us. Most of the blue colour is scattered out before it reaches your eyes. The red and orange light is what's left and it sometimes paints the sky with stunning colours.

Kaleidoscope

WHAT YOU NEED

paints and brush

scissors

mirror card

black paper

card

cellophane bag

glue

sequins

stapler

1 Make a long triangular box shape from the mirror card, with the reflective side facing inwards.

2 Make a card tube that the triangular box will fit into. Paint and decorate with bright colours.

3 Put a selection of sequins into a small cellophane bag. Staple to close and glue to one end of the tube.

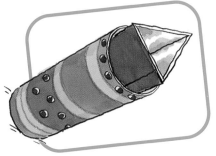

4 Insert the triangular box into the tube. Cut a circle of black paper slightly bigger than the end of the tube, and make a hole in the middle.

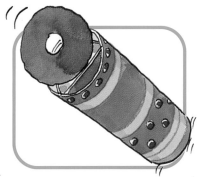

5 Stick the black paper over the end of the tube and trim to fit. Shake and turn the kaleidoscope, and look through the hole in the end to see the different patterns it creates.

Twist and turn and watch the colours sparkle!

Flashing neons

Have you ever seen brightly coloured neon signs lighting up a city centre at night? These thin tubes of light are used on advertising signs and make a dazzling display. Unlike normal lights, they are made using thin tubes that can be easily shaped into words and pictures. The tubes are filled with a gas that gives off a glowing light when electricity is sent through it.

NEW ENERGY

Neon is one of the gases found in the atmosphere, the mixture of gases that surrounds the Earth.

The word neon comes from the ancient Greek word for 'new'. When electricity travels through a glass tube filled with neon gas, it gives energy to the very tiny particles that make up the gas. As the electricity streams from one end of the tube to the other, it hits the particles of neon. This gives them more energy – just as a billiard ball is given more energy when it is hit by another billiard ball. But instead of the moving energy of a billiard ball, the neon particles give out their new energy as a glowing light, which we can see.

COLOUR CHANGE

If the tubes are filled with other gases, different coloured lights can be made. Neon gas gives out a strong orange-red glow. Helium gas gives a golden-yellow light, and krypton gas shines pale violet. When sodium vapour gas is used, it makes a vivid yellow light, which is often used in street lights.

City lights

Colour

WHAT YOU NEED

paints and brush

grey card

glue

black mounting card

white pencil

scissors

1 Draw with the white pencil, two outlines of skyscrapers – draw the tallest on dark grey card, and lower buildings on lighter grey. Cut them out.

2 Use paint to create lighted windows.

Brightly shining lights for a city that never sleeps!

3 Stick the tallest layer of skyscrapers onto a piece of mounting card.

PVA

4 Fold the bottom of the lower row of skyscrapers and glue onto the top of the 1st layer, creating a 3D effect. Add sticky tape to secure in place.

PVA

Black and white

REFLECT OR ABSORB

The colour of the Earth's surface affects the way it reflects or absorbs the heat of the Sun. A white surface of snow or ice reflects back about 90 per cent of the Sun's heat. This makes snowy places, such as the Arctic and Antarctic, even colder than they already are. Black surfaces, such as a tarmac road, reflect only about 5 per cent of the Sun's heat and absorb the rest. This is why they get so hot on a sunny day and may even melt to form sticky tar. Animals that live in cold places, such as Arctic butterflies, often have dark colours to help them absorb heat from the Sun and stay warm.

The squares on this chessboard are black and white to help separate them clearly. Black and white are special colours. The black squares look so dark because black takes in, or absorbs, nearly all the colours in light. The white squares look so pale because white reflects all the colours in light.

SEEING IN BLACK AND WHITE

Did you know that many animals, such as dogs, cats, horses and cows, cannot see the colours we see? They see the world in shades of black and white and grey. Almost all people see in full colour. Our relatives, the apes and monkeys also see in colour. Other animals with colour vision include reptiles, such as snakes and lizards, and birds, butterflies, bees and many fishes.

18

Chalk and charcoal designs

Make dramatic pictures by using only black and white

2 Use your finger to smudge the patterns in places.

1 Make several pictures using charcoal on white paper, and chalk on black paper. Draw big, bold, unusual patterns — use your imagination!

3 Mount on card.

Make a display of your chalk and charcoal pictures.

19

Invisible rays

Sunlight brightens up the day. But it can also burn your skin if you are not careful. Visible light is what you see, but the Sun also gives off light rays that you can't see. The heat you feel from the Sun comes from invisible infra-red rays. A suntan, or worse, sunburn, comes from invisible ultra-violet rays.

INFRA-RED AND ULTRA-VIOLET LIGHT

When all the colours in a ray of sunlight are separated they make a rainbow of colours called a spectrum. The spectrum has a band of red on one edge and a band of violet on the other edge. Beyond each end of the spectrum are the invisible rays of light. Infra-red means below red and ultra-violet means beyond violet.

FEEL THE HEAT

All hot things give off infra-red rays – and the warmer they get the more infra-red rays they give off. Special pieces of electronic equipment can pick up infra-red rays and turn them into colours that we can see. The hottest areas look yellow and the coldest areas look blue.

DANGEROUS RAYS

Ultra-violet, or UV, rays are dangerous because they can pass through the outer layer of your skin and burn the flesh underneath. Too many of them may cause skin cancer. A brown pigment called melanin – which turns the skin brown – helps to protect the skin from the harmful effects of ultra-violet light.

A BEE'S EYE-VIEW

Even though we can't see ultra-violet light, insects such as bees can. A bee's-eye view of a flower is very different from the view you see. The ultra-violet light reflected back from the flower makes it stand out far more so the bee can find it easily.

This is how a bee sees a flower – in ultra violet light.

Colour

WHAT YOU NEED

scissors

ribbon

card

paper

paints and brush

glitter

string

glue

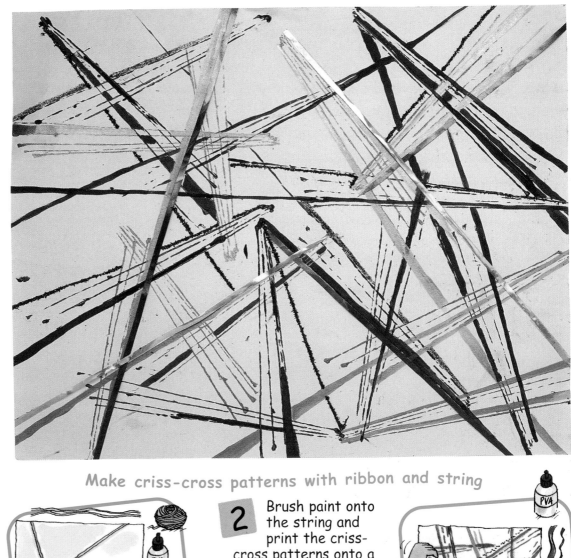

Make criss-cross patterns with ribbon and string

1 Cut long lengths of string and stick onto a piece of card.

2 Brush paint onto the string and print the criss-cross patterns onto a piece of white paper.

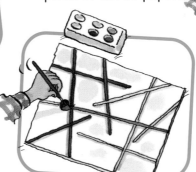

3 Add lines of glitter, paint and lengths of ribbon to your string print picture.

21

I spy

The way we see a colour is affected by the other colours around it. The same colour can look lighter or darker when it is placed against a different coloured background. For instance, the central green square in this painting 'stands out' because it is framed by ever-increasing shades of blue. If we changed the colours around the green square, the picture would look very different.

Imagine you are eating a cheese and tomato sandwich. The cheese looks yellow because it reflects yellow light. The tomato looks red because it reflects red light. The other rainbow colours in light are absorbed by the cheese and the tomato so we can't see them. We see different colours because of the way different things reflect light. The secret of how we can see in colour is found in the millions of tiny cone-shaped nerve endings at the back of the eye. You have three types of cones, which respond to red, green or blue light. Light from the cheese would affect the green and red cones because mixing green and red light makes yellow light.

COLOUR BLINDNESS

When something goes wrong with the cones in our eyes, the messages about light colours don't get through to the brain. This causes colour blindness. Colour-blind people find it hard to tell the difference between certain colours, especially red, green and grey.

TRICK OF THE LIGHT

Puzzle pictures or optical illusions can also trick the brain. In these cases, what we think we see is not what is actually there. Sometimes, these images may have two or more possible meanings. The brain cannot decide which one to choose, so we see first one meaning and then the other.

Puzzle picture

WHAT YOU NEED

paints and brush

paper

pencil

1 Draw a small star shape in the corner of a piece of paper.

2 Now draw some smaller shapes inside the star shape.

Can you spot the star hidden among the shapes?

3 Cover the rest of the paper with more shapes.

4 Colour in all the shapes with brightly coloured paints.

23

Shadowy shapes

Have you ever played the game 'catch my shadow' with your friends? You have to try and stand on each other's shadow. You need a sunny day for this game because your shadow will only appear when your body stops sunlight from reaching the ground.

LIGHT RAYS

Light travels in straight lines called light rays. As long as nothing is in the way, the light rays move in one direction. But when light rays hit an object, they are stopped. This leaves a dark space on the other side of the object called a shadow. On cloudy days, you will not have a shadow because the clouds soak up some of the sunlight and scatter the rest in all directions. All the sunlight has to move in one direction for shadows to form.

LIGHT AND MATERIALS

Shadows form when light falls on materials that do not let the light go through them. These are called opaque materials. Wood, metal and your body are opaque. Other materials, such as air, water and clear glass, let light travel through them. These are called transparent. Some materials, such as frosted glass, let a little light go through them. These are called translucent.

In this play, dancing puppets cast shadows on a lit-up screen.

Puppet theatre

Colour

WHAT YOU NEED

paints and brush

tape

scissors

pencil

sticks

black card

tracing paper

glitter

cardboard box

1 Cut out all four sides of the box as shown.

2 Paint red curtains at the front of the theatre, and paint the sides and top using plain colours.

3 Cut a panel as shown. Paint and decorate with glitter, then tape to the top of the theatre.

4 Draw a variety of animal and people shapes on black card and cut out.

5 Tape the characters onto wooden sticks.

6 Tape tracing paper onto the inside of the front of the theatre. Then shine a light at the back of the box, and use the open sides to operate your puppets.

The puppets' shadows will create a dramatic effect!

25

Laser beams

The most extraordinary light of all comes from a laser. It punches through steel, carries telephone signals over long distances, is used by surgeons, plays compact discs, reads the bar codes at supermarket tills and lights up the sky with amazing patterns at a concert.

LIGHT ENERGY

A laser is a machine that produces a narrow beam of very bright light. Laser light does not spread out like ordinary light, so it is very powerful. It can travel steadily in a direct path over huge distances.

A laser light show at a rock concert.

HOLOGRAMS

A hologram is a type of photograph that is made when two laser beams cross each other. It is made with light on glass instead of with colours on paper like an ordinary photograph. A hologram is very special because it looks like a three-dimensional solid object. If you walk round a hologram, it looks different from every angle, just like a real object. The reason holograms look so real is that they are accurate recordings of the light reflected from an object. Holograms are very difficult to forge, or copy, so they are used on credit cards, bank cheques and even concert tickets.

Silver torch

Colour

WHAT YOU NEED

torch

card tube

foil

paints and brush

scissors

tissue paper

sequins

glue

1 Cover the torch with a cardboard tube, but cut out a hole around the on/off button.

2 Paint and decorate the cardboard tube with strips of foil, tissue paper and sequins.

PVA

3 Place the tube over the handle of the torch and stuff the open end with ripped tissue paper to hold in place.

27

Tints and dyes

Look at the clothes hanging in your wardrobe. They will be made of cotton, wool, nylon or other different fabrics. Many of these fabrics may be bright and colourful, with interesting patterns or designs, but almost all would have started as plain white material. All the colours and designs have been added by dyeing or tinting the fabric. A dye is a chemical that changes the colour of something. A tint changes a colour to a different shade.

Natural or synthetic

Dyes come from natural sources, such as the roots or berries of plants. Artificial or synthetic dyes were developed by scientists and are now more widely used than natural dyes. Before it can work, the dye is usually dissolved in a 'dye bath' full of a special liquid. When the fabric is added, its fibres absorb the tiny molecules of dye and it changes colour. To stop the colour from fading, a substance called a mordant can be added. This combines with the dye molecules to fix them into the fabric to make it 'colour fast'.

Colour

Tie-dye a T-shirt

Experiment to create different tie-dye patterns

1 Spread out newspaper to protect the work area. Wrap rubber bands round sections of T-shirt.

2 Make the dye in a bowl or bucket. Wearing rubber gloves, put the T-shirt in the dye. Follow the instructions on the packet.

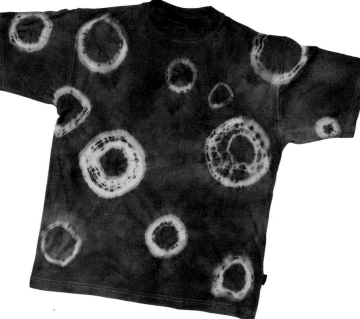

3 Remove the T-shirt from the dye and run it under cold water until the water is running clear from it.

4 Remove the rubber bands and leave the T-shirt to dry.

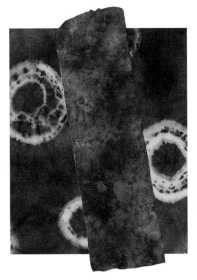

You can create different patterns by wrapping the rubber bands in different ways. Experiment on scraps of fabric to get the effect you want. You could also try:

- scrunching the fabric
- knotting the fabric
- folding the fabric
- wrapping the fabric around pebbles

Tie-dyeing can be messy so ask an adult to help

Lots of dots

Pixels in close up on a television screen.

If you look at the picture on a colour television from really close up, you will see that it is made up of lots of red, blue and green dots. There are about 350,000 of these dots and they are called pixels, which is short for picture elements. From a distance, the dots merge together so they look like one picture in full colour.

FROM CAMERA TO SCREEN

A colour television camera converts the picture it takes into electrical signals. These are then changed into radio waves, which are sent through the air to the television set. The television set works in the opposite way to the television camera, changing the radio waves first into electrical signals and then into a pattern of coloured light. This pattern is the picture you see on your television screen.

MIXING LIGHT

All the colours you see on a TV screen are made by mixing red, blue and green light. These are the primary colours of light. Light colours do not mix in the same way as paint colours. Red and green light mix to make yellow. Blue and green light make cyan (bluish-green). Red and blue light make magenta (purplish-red). And all the colours of light mixed together make white. What colour do you get if you mix the primary colours of paint (red, blue and yellow) together?

SPLITTING AND MIXING

A television camera splits the light from an image into the three primary colours. Each colour goes to a different camera tube, which converts the light into electrical signals. Inside a television is an electron gun with three tubes, one for each colour. The gun fires electrical signals at the back of the television screen, which is coated with strips of chemicals called phosphors. When the electrical signals hit the phosphors, they glow red, green or blue to make the coloured picture.

Colour

Spot painting

Mix colours and make pretty patterns in this dotty picture!

powder paints

brush

white paper

acrylic

pencil

mounting card

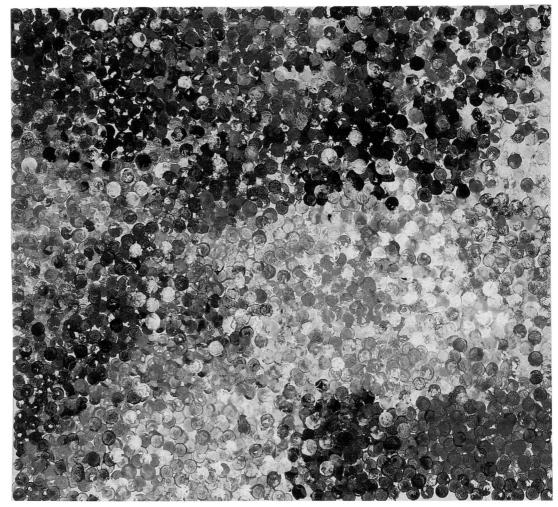

1 Use the end of the pencil to dip into different coloured paints and print onto white paper.

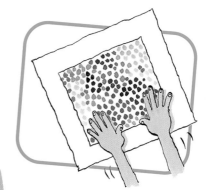

2 When the page is covered with lots of dots, leave the picture to dry and mount it on thick card.

Floating bubbles

Have you ever tried to blow a water bubble? Bubbles without soap won't work. You need the soap to make the water particles stretch apart long enough to form a bubble. The soap particles help to stop the water in the bubble from escaping – and bursting the bubble. A bubble expert once kept a bubble for 340 days, but most people's bubbles pop much sooner than that!

Bubble shapes

Bubbles are usually rounded shapes called spheres. This is because the particles that make up the bubble liquid like to stick together. Each particle pulls on the ones next to it, making a shape with the smallest possible surface area for its size. This happens to be a sphere. A sphere has a smaller surface area than other shapes, such as cubes and cylinders.

Bubble colours

One of the most beautiful things about bubbles is their shimmering rainbow colours. These colours come from the way light is reflected from the inner and outer surfaces of the bubbles. Light reflected from the inside of the soap bubble travels a longer distance than the light reflected from the outside of the bubble. When the inside and outside reflections meet, the different colours in the light interfere with each other, creating the coloured patterns. These are called interference colours.

Bubble prints

Colour

mounting card

paper

straw

paint

washing-up liquid

spoon

bowl

1 In the bowl, mix together a small amount of water, washing-up liquid and a squirt of paint.

2 Blow into it through the straw, creating coloured bubbles.

3 Lay a piece of paper over the top of the bowl, and lift the bubble pattern onto the surface of the paper.

When dry, mount your pictures.

4

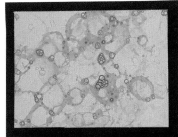
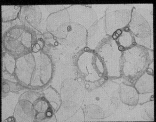
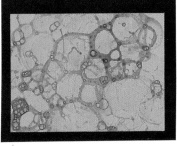

Blow bubbles, and see amazing patterns appear!

Firecrackers

Bang! Whizzzz! Whooop! Fizzz! The sky is suddenly filled with bright patterns of coloured light as rockets explode high overhead. Catherine wheels whirl around, throwing out showers of sparkling stars, and golden and silver 'rain' cascades to the ground. Where do all the fantastic colours in fireworks come from?

BURNING-METAL EFFECTS

Firework colours are produced when different metals in the fireworks burn with different coloured flames. Magnesium metal makes a brilliant white light when it burns, sodium burns with a yellowish-orange colour, copper and barium give off a bluish-green colour, lithium and strontium burn red, and potassium makes fireworks violet.

ROCKET SCIENCE

Firework rockets are packed with gunpowder, which burns super-hot and very quickly, especially when it is packed into a thin cardboard tube. As the powder burns, smoke and hot gases stream down from the bottom of the rocket and push the rocket up into the sky. The long stick attached to the tube keeps the rocket flying in a straight line. Eventually, the burning powder sets fire to an explosive charge that makes glowing stars shoot out of the end of the rocket. Sometimes, the gunpowder is mixed with chemicals and packed in separate layers. Each layer gives off a different colour as the layers explode one after the other.

Colour

Firework display

silver and gold paint

black paper

brush

glitter

glue

pastels

1 Make small dots of pastel on the paper and smudge them with your finger.

2 Add spots of silver and gold paint. Spread on glue in swirls and sprinkle with glitter.

Add swirls of glow-paint to make your display shine in the dark

Colour and mood

Colours can say a lot, without any words. They can change our mood – the way we feel. Red, orange and yellow are said to be 'warm' colours and they can make us feel cheerful and excited. The sun glows yellow and orange. Blues and greens, on the other hand, are thought of as 'cool' colours, which give us calm, secure feelings. People cool off in the shade of green trees or go for a refreshing dip in the blue-green sea.

DECORATING COLOURS

The colours people choose when they are decorating their homes can change the feel of the rooms. Pale shades of 'cool' colours make rooms feel spacious and peaceful, while 'warm' colours make rooms feel friendly and cosy. Dark colours can have a shrinking effect, making rooms appear smaller and high ceilings feel lower.

COLOURS AND FOOD

How would you feel if you had to eat blue rice or purple pizza? The colour of our food is almost as important as its taste. Some frozen or tinned foods have artificial colour added to them so we will want to eat them. The colour of food often tells us whether it will be good to eat. Fresh vegetables are green, while old vegetables turn yellow and brown.

Artists use different colours to change the mood of the viewer. How does this painting make you feel?

Soft-glow lampshade

1 On card, draw a big circle with a smaller circle in the middle. Cut out.

2 Cut out shapes with a craft knife. Then paint the frame of the lampshade in gold.

This colourful lampshade will give your bedroom a warm and cosy feeling

3 Glue strips of different coloured tissue paper on the inside of the shade. Trim the tissue paper, so that a different colour shows through each hole.

4 Bend the two ends of the shade round and tape together.

5 Make a wire circle, with a straight piece across the middle, as shown. Attach this to the top of the shade. Ask an adult to hang it from the light.

Rolls of film

Smile, please! It's fun taking pictures and nice to have photographs to remind you of special events, people and places. The word 'photography' means 'writing with light' and a photograph is a copy of a pattern of light that you can look at again and again.

How a camera works

A camera works in much the same way as your eyes. It has a lens that collects all the light from a scene and bends it so that it falls on the film to form a picture, or image. Both the eye and a camera control the amount of light that goes into the image. The camera does this by changing the size of a hole, called the aperture, and the amount of time a flap, called the shutter, stays open to let light into the camera.

Developing and printing

When you have taken all the pictures on a film, they are turned into prints. The film is dipped in chemicals to stop it being sensitive to light. These make the light colours on the film appear dark and the dark colours appear light. The developed film is called a negative because it is a reverse of the real image. To make the print, light is shone through the negative onto special paper. When the light hits the chemicals on this paper, the light and dark areas of the negative are turned back to their real colour on the paper.

Cartoon snapshots

Make negatives of your own special scenes

Stick images onto the back of the black frames to create your film.

1 Make several frames from black paper. Cut holes, as shown, so the frames look like camera film.

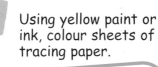

2 Using yellow paint or ink, colour sheets of tracing paper.

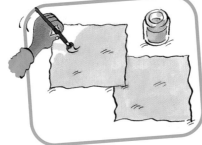

3 Use black paint to create images on the yellow background.

Magic glass

NEWTON'S PRISM

Newton suggested that the prism had split the light into red, orange, yellow, green, blue, indigo and violet light. At the time, most other scientists thought that the prism added something to the light to make the colours. Newton showed that sunlight is really a mixture of light of different colours.

COLOUR PATHS

When light travels through a prism, each of the colours moves at a slightly different speed. This makes the path of each colour 'bend' by a different amount. As the colours leave the prism, each one follows a different path, so each colour is separate. If the coloured light passes through a second prism, the colours are 'bent' back together again so the light shining out of the prism has no colour. This is called white light.

Over 300 years ago, a scientist called Isaac Newton did some experiments. He held a thick triangle of glass, called a prism, in front of a thin beam of sunlight. He put some white paper in front of the prism and saw a rainbow of colours, called a spectrum, shining onto the paper.

BENDING LIGHT

Light always travels in straight lines. It does not really bend. But when light goes through water or glass, it seems to bend. This is called refraction. What really happens is that the light slows down when it hits the water or glass. This makes it change direction and head off at a different angle – so it looks as if it is bending.

Colour

Make a model prism, and see all the colours of light

WHAT YOU NEED

wire

bubble wrap and cling film

tissue paper

foil

tracing paper

glue

1 Make a multi-panelled frame of triangles from the wire as shown.

2 Cover all the sides by glueing on the see-through materials you have collected — bubble wrap, cling film, tracing paper, etc.

3 Glue a strip of silver foil between two panels. On another panel glue white tissue, followed by strips of rainbow-patterned tissue.

PVA

41

Clear crystals

Glittering and sparkling in the light, the smooth, shiny sides of clear crystals reflect all the colours of the rainbow. Crystals come in a variety of shapes, sizes and colours, but they all have a repetitive pattern, whatever their shape. Crystals grow naturally in the rocks beneath the Earth's surface.

MINERALS

Our whole planet is built from minerals. These are natural, non-living materials. Some are precious and rare, such as diamonds. Others, like quartz, are found almost everywhere.

EARTH'S ROCK JEWELS

All minerals form in magma – the hot, molten rock under the Earth's surface. Most minerals make crystal shapes. There are six basic crystal shapes and most crystals have a specific colour. Many gemstones are crystals that have been cut and polished. Rare gems, such as rubies and emeralds, are very precious.

PRISMS AND PYRAMIDS

Crystals grow into shapes called prisms with flat, smooth, shiny sides and sharp corners. Sometimes the prisms have flat ends, sometimes they have pyramid-shaped ends. Quartz always forms crystals with six-sided prisms and six-sided pyramid ends. Salt always forms cube-shaped crystals. Some crystals are so perfectly shaped, they look as if a machine has cut them – but they are completely natural!

COLOURS AND LIGHT

Crystals such as pure quartz are clear and colourless. But when another material mixes with a growing crystal it can colour it yellow, purple, pink or brown. Coloured crystals may be very beautiful and are often used in jewellery. We call crystals like these gemstones.

Quartz mobile

Hang your shining crystal by the window so it reflects the light

Colour

WHAT YOU NEED

sequins

foil

buttons

clingfilm

nylon

tracing paper

beads

scissors

wire

gold thread

1 Make a frame as shown from the wire.

2 Wrap with twisted lengths of foil.

3 Thread sequins, buttons, plastic beads, etc., onto lengths of gold thread or nylon, with a needle.

Attach these lengths to the top of your crystal so they dangle down the middle when it is hung up.

4

5 Cover sides with cling film and tracing paper, then decorate the outside with sequins.

PVA

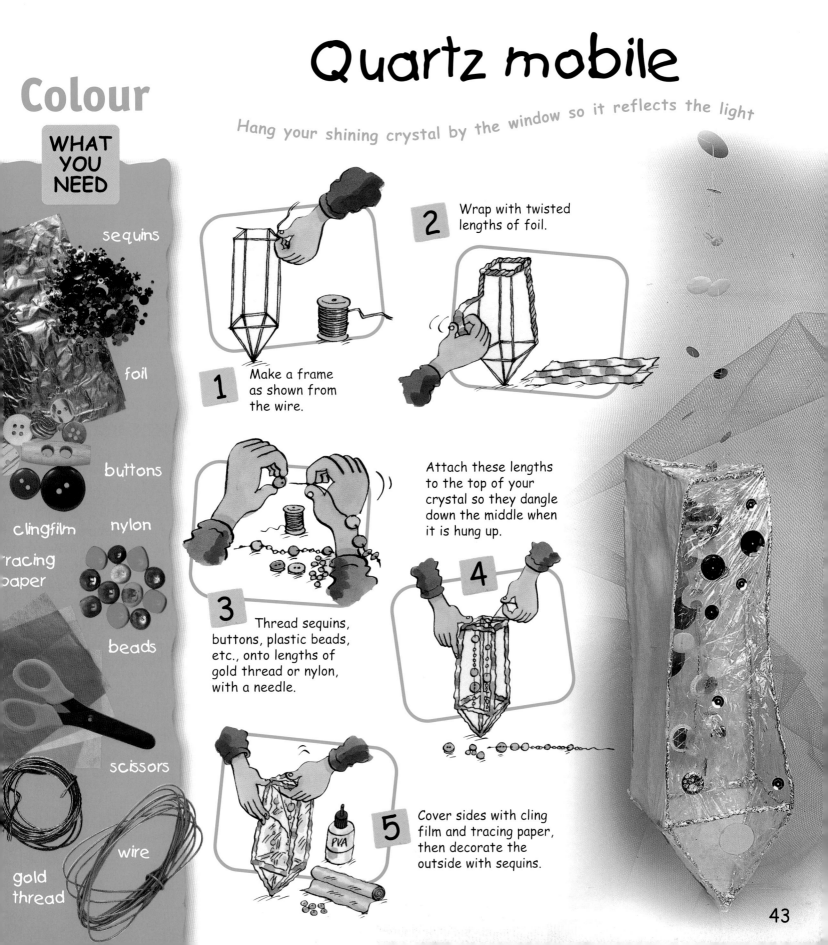

Lamps and lanterns

All over the world, light and colour are an important part of festivals. Lamps and lanterns may guide visiting goddesses, welcome the spirits of the dead or remind people of events that happened long ago. Colours make occasions, such as the coming of spring, new year or independence days, even more special.

FESTIVAL OF LIGHTS

In late October or early November, people of the Hindu religion celebrate the Festival of Lights, called Diwali. Before sunset, people set out rows of Diwali lamps outside their front doors, on windowsills or on the roofs. Diwali means 'row of lights'. Hindus believe that the lights help to guide the goddess Lakshmi, who brings good luck to the family in the house for the next year.

WELCOMING LANTERNS

In July, Japanese Buddhists celebrate the Festival of Bon, also called the Festival of Lanterns. They remember those who have died by placing a lighted lantern at the door to welcome the spirits into their homes. On the last day, people light paper lanterns, set them on wooden floats and put them in the water. As they drift into the dark, the tiny lantern boats carry the spirits on their way to the other world.

Colour

Chinese lanterns

WHAT YOU NEED

paints and brush

sequins

scissors

tape

paper

glue

string

1 Fold a piece of paper in half lengthwise.

2 Cut out a series of shapes from the paper.

3 Open the paper out, paint and decorate with sequins.

PVA

4 Tape the two outer edges of the paper together to create a cylinder shape.

5 Tape a length of string or cotton inside the top of the lantern to hang it up.

Hang your lanterns all around the house to make it look cheerful and festive

45

Glossary and Index

mirror 10

molecule A very small particle containing two or more atoms. 14

mordant A substance which can be added to dyes to make them stay in the material. 28

mosaic 5

negative A reversed image created when light hits the special film placed in a camera. 38

neon gas A colourless gas found in small quantities in the atmosphere. It is used to fill some electric light bulbs. 16

opaque Not transparent. Does not transmit or reflect light. 6, 24

optical illusion A false message sent to the brain by the eye. 22

orange 14, 16, 36

particle A name for a very small part of a substance. Atom and electrons are kinds of particle. 14, 16, 32

pattern 8, 12, 26, 30, 32, 38, 42

phosphors A substance which glows with light when it is charged with electricity. 30

photosynthesis Process by which plants use sunlight to convert water and carbon dioxide gas into food. 6, 18

pixels The tiny parts that make up a whole picture, for example on a television or computer screen, or in a photograph. 30

potassium A metal which reacts violently with water and air. 34

primary colour The colours red, blue and yellow, which can be mixed together in different combinations to make almost any other colour. 4, 30

prism A transparent polygon-shaped, such as a triangle or pyramid, solid object, which bends light and splits white light into its coloured spectrum. 8, 40

quartz A transparent and colourless mineral that is found in many rocks of the Earth. 42

rainbow 14, 20, 32, 40, 42

red 4, 14, 16, 22, 30, 36

reflection Bouncing back of a light or sound wave as it hits a surface. 10, 12, 18, 20, 22, 32

refraction Bending of a light ray or sound wave as it passes from one substance to another different substance, for example air to water, or air to a prism. 8, 40

ruby A precious stone that is mined from minerals in the Earth. 42

secondary colour A colour made by mixing two primary colours together. 4

shade A colour that varies slightly from a standard colour. A shade is made by mixing black with a colour. 4, 8, 28

shadow The dark area or shape cast on a surface where an opaque object blocks out light rays. 6, 24

shutter A closing mechanism used in cameras to control how much light can enter. 38

silver 8, 12

sodium A silver white element of many metals. 16, 34

spectrum The rainbow colours, red, orange, yellow, green, blue, indigo and violet, that make up white light. 8, 36, 20, 40

steel 12

Sun 6, 14, 18, 20, 24

tint A shade of a colour. A tint is made by mixing white with a colour. 4, 28

tone A shade of a colour. A tone is made by mixing grey with a colour. 4

translucent Semi-transparent. Allows light to partially pass through it. 6, 24

transparent See-through. Allows light to pass through it. 6, 24

ultra-violet (UV) rays 20

violet 14, 16

virtual image An image that appears to be somewhere that it actually is not, such as a reflection from a mirror. 10, 12

visible light Light that can be seen. 20

white 18, 30

white light All the colours of the spectrum blended together. Sunlight is white light. 40

yellow 4, 14, 16, 22, 30, 36